MW01128730

a kids book about

BRAIN HEALTH

by Dr. Krystal L. Culler & LeAnne Stuver
in partnership with the **Virtual Brain Health Center**

a
kids
book
about

Text and design copyright © 2023
by A Kids Book About, Inc.

Copyright is good! It ensures that work like this can exist, and more work in the future can be created.

All rights reserved. No part of this publication may be reproduced, distributed, or transmitted in any form or by any means, including photocopying, recording, other electronic or mechanical methods, without the prior written permission of the publisher, except in the case of brief quotations embodied in critical reviews and certain other noncommercial uses permitted by copyright law. For permission requests, write to the publisher.

A Kids Book About, Kids Are Ready, and the colophon 'a' are trademarks of A Kids Book About, Inc.

Printed in the United States of America.

A Kids Book About books are available online: *akidsco.com*

To share your stories, ask questions, or inquire about bulk purchases (schools, libraries, and nonprofits), please use the following email address: *hello@akidsco.com*

Print ISBN: 978-1-958825-75-4
Ebook ISBN: 978-1-958825-76-1

Designed by Rick DeLucco
Edited by Emma Wolf

better together*

*This book is best read together, grownup and kid.

 akidsco.com

a kids
book
about

This book honors the many individuals, families, and organizations who have shared their brain health journeys with us. Your insights have influenced this book and will impact those who read it by helping them understand and prioritize brain health for themselves and for every one of us.

To my awe-inspiring niece, Teagan Grace, whose actions illuminate that kids can create the greatest ripples in promoting healthy brains! – Aunt Krystal

Intro

Have you talked to your kids about brain health? If not, it's never too late—most grownups haven't. In fact, most grownups don't really know how to even start a conversation about brain health with the kids in their lives.

Some families are forced to talk about it when a loved one is diagnosed with a brain injury or disease. But you do not have to wait for a difficult time to start the discussion with your kids—in fact, we prefer you don't wait.

We want **everyone** to talk about brain health, every single day!

In this book, we define brain health, teach you some brainy facts, and help you learn what a brain-healthy lifestyle looks like.

Now, let's talk brain health!

Have you thought about
your brain today?

Like, really thought about it?

Most of the time, we don't notice it unless something feels wrong.

Like if you have a headache, or trouble concentrating, or a brain freeze from eating ice cream too fast!

The truth is, **our brain is involved in EVERY**

Everything we think.

Everything we feel.

Every decision we make.

It all begins and ends with the brain.

So, our brain health really matters.

Now, you might be wondering,
what is brain health?

Essentially, brain health
is how your brain thrives.

And all the things that are a part of your brain health might surprise you!

connecting, focus,

breathing, memory,

attention,

sensing,

thinking,

feeling, learning,

sleeping, moving,

decision-making,

concentrating,

laughing,

hydrating,

talking,

problem-solving,

planning,

relaxing, eating,

playing, and more!

Brain health is about the balance between keeping the brain...

active

and keeping it
calm.

Your brain is

ZING.

(Just like you.)

It's constantly growing
new brain cells, or **neurons.**

And, your brain changes based on
your behaviors, lifestyle, and habits.

This is called **neuroplasticity.** Basically, the brain is elastic and fantastic!

When we say elastic, we mean it can stretch to learn.

We have a powerful ability
to help our brains grow.

All brains are unique.

No 2 are the same.

Our thoughts, emotions, actions, and environment can all impact our brains and how they develop.

Brain health is about taking care of *your exceptional brain* so you can do all the things you love.

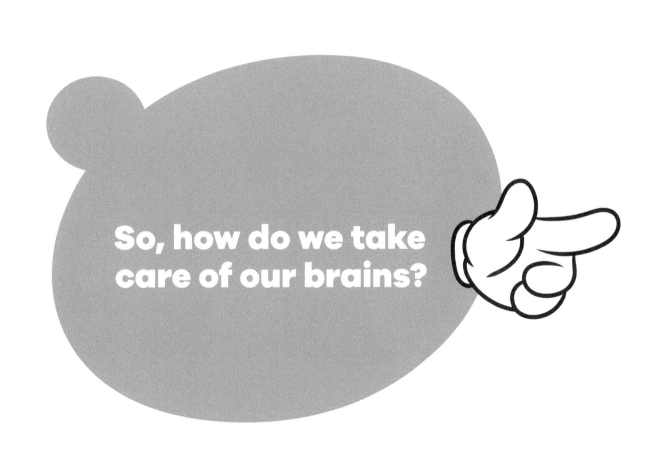

There's a lot you can do to keep your brain healthy and strong!

Your body is meant to

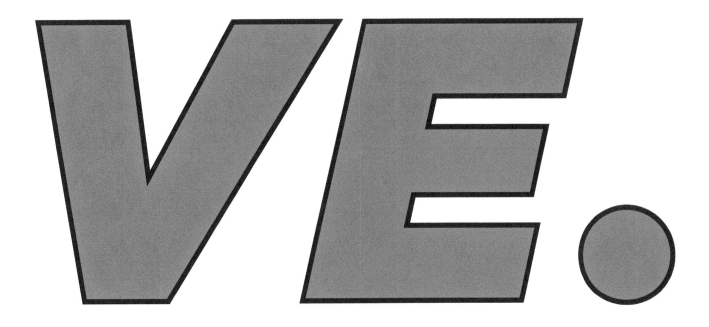

VE.

But did you know your
brain should, too?

Yep, your body and brain work best when they are active.

There are many ways
to move your body—

walking,

dancing,

jumping,

rolling,

and more!

Just like we exercise our bodies, we need to exercise our brains every day, too.

And here are some ways to do that!

Ask about the world around you, stay curious, and keep exploring things that are interesting.

Do things that help your brain stay strong like reading books, solving puzzles, and going on adventures.

It also helps to talk about the feelings you have with people you trust.

We don't just feel happy things; sometimes, we feel sad, frustrated, or scared.

But ALL of your feelings matter, and it helps your brain when you share what you're experiencing.

Your brain requires a lot of energy.

It's important to drink plenty of water and eat nutritious foods throughout the day.

Your brain also needs to rest and relax.

is necessary to function well.

Short naps during the day can help
give your brain a boost in energy!

And rest doesn't always mean sleep.

It's important to take

BREAKS

throughout the day.

This can look like:

spending time with your pet,

listening to music,

stretching,

practicing mindfulness,

or getting some fresh air.*

*Kids, you're usually pretty good at knowing when you need a break! Your grownups may need some help with this.

All the things we just talked about are mental and emotional protection for our brains.

And, physical protection matters too!

Wear your seatbelt in the car, and wear a helmet to protect your head when it needs it, and when you bike, scooter, or skateboard.

If you hit your head
hard enough to say,
"OU

Each of us gets 1 brain,

and no matter how old or young
we are, it's important to protect it.

Some people think that brain health is just for grownups.

R, people think brain health is important only when something feels wrong.

But brain health

EVERY

is for...

TONE!

Your brain needs care every day.

And it's never too early or too late to pay attention to your brain!

And here's something super important...

There's no health without brain health. It impacts your whole self.

Your brain health is up to you!

You can make choices every day to keep your brain active and healthy.

Practice **gratitude***
and be kind to your mind.

*Practicing gratitude means actively being thankful for something (like our amazing brains!).

Thank your brain every day for all the wonderful things it does for you!

IT'S PRETTY INCRE (AND SO

Outro

May this book spark a lifelong conversation of ways to nurture your one-and-only, brilliant brain. (Please revisit this book with your kids again...and again...and again!)

Your brain health matters. Your brain care is nonnegotiable.

Here are a few simple ways to take charge of your brain health.

Keep your brain top of mind.
Commit to at least one, daily, brain-boosting action—connect, move, nourish, learn, and more!

Keep trying new things.
Practice simple, doable, daily brain care rituals like mindful breathing, gratitude, or brain breaks, which promote restfulness and relaxation.

Keep talking about your brain health.
Share what you are doing for your daily brain care with your kids and loved ones. And ask your kids about their brains, too.

Your commitment to brain care sends ripples of positive change to your family and community. Together, we build better brains.

About The Authors

Meet the brains behind this book.

Dr. Krystal L. Culler (she/her) is a doctor of behavioral health and the trailblazing founder of the Virtual Brain Health Center. She was a super serious kid who asked A LOT of questions, and she still does! (Just ask her mom and husband.)

LeAnne Stuver (she/her) is a dedicated nurse educator fueled by a passion for empowering others to embrace a brain-healthy lifestyle. She transitioned her childhood love of reading books about animals (mostly horses) to a career in healthcare and lifelong learning.

Together, through their Virtual Brain Health Center, they champion initiatives and support projects that share brain care worldwide to support kids, grownups, and caregivers alike.

 @virtualbrainhealthcenter   virtualbrainhealthcenter.com

 @virtualbrainhealthcenter   @virtualbrainhealthcenter

a kids book about MONEY
by Stramwasser

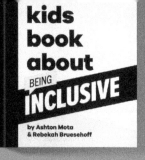
kids book about BEING INCLUSIVE
by Ashton Mota & Rebekah Bruesehoff

kids book about diversity
by Chyanne Gordon

kids book about LEADErSHIP
by Orion Jean

kids book about IMMIGR
by MJ Calderon

a kids book about SAFETY
by Soraya Sutherlin, CEM
in partnership with JUDY

a kids book about CLIMATE CHANGE
by Zanagee Artis & Olivia Greenspan

a kids book about IMAGINATION
by LEVAR BURTON

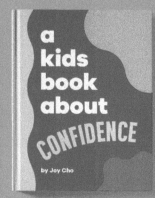
a kids book about CONFIDENCE
by Joy Cho

a kids book about S
by Eve

a kids book about ANXIETY
by Happy Faces

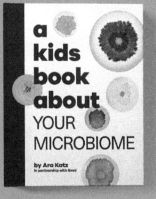
a kids book about YOUR MICROBIOME
by Ara Katz
in partnership with Seed

a kids book about racism
by Jelani Memory

a kids book about DISABILITIES
by Kristine Napper

a kids book about boredom
by Kyleste

a kids book about DIVORCE
by Ashley Simpo

a kids book about cancer
by Dr. Kelsie Storm & Sarah Porter

a kids book about BEING TRANSGENDER
by Gia Parr
in partnership with The GenderCool Project

a kids book about DEPRESSION
by Kileah McIlvain

a kids book about
by Meir

a kids book about SHAME

a kids book about THE TULSA

Discover more at akidsco.com

Printed in the USA
CPSIA information can be obtained
at www.ICGtesting.com
LVHW072327281023
762269LV00004B/4